# JOURNAL

PETER PAUPER PRESS, INC.
RYE BROOK, NEW YORK

## PETER PAUPER PRESS
*Fine Books and Gifts Since 1928*

### Our Company

In 1928, at the age of twenty-two, Peter Beilenson began printing books on a small press in the basement of his parents' home in Larchmont, New York. Peter—and later his wife, Edna—sought to create fine books that sold at "prices even a pauper could afford."

Today, still family owned and operated, Peter Pauper Press continues to honor our founders' legacy—and our customers' expectations—of beauty, quality, and value.

Cover art: Réunion des Musées Nationaux/Art Resource, NY
Elaborate gold-tooled binding, seventeenth-century France.

Designed by Eleanor Kostyk

Visit us at www.peterpauper.com